Prairie Schooner Book Prize in Poetry
Editor Kwame Dawes

Fetish: Poems

Orlando Ricardo Menes

University of Nebraska Press | Lincoln and London

Acknowledgments for the use of copyrighted material appear on page xi, which constitutes an extension of the copyright page.

Library of Congress Cataloging-in-Publication Data
Menes, Orlando Ricardo.
[Poems. Selections]
Fetish: poems / Orlando Ricardo Menes.
pages; cm.—(Prairie Schooner book prize in poetry)
ISBN 978-0-8032-6491-5 (pbk.: alk. paper)
I. Title.
PS3563.E52F48 2013
811'.54—dc23   2013007125

Set in Arno Pro by Laura Wellington.
Designed by J. Vadnais.

for my wife Ivis and
our two children,
Valerie and Adrian

From my North of cold whistled in a sepulchral South,
Her South of pine and coral and coralline sea,
Her home, not mine, in the ever-freshened Keys . . . .
—Wallace Stevens, "Farewell to Florida"

In dusk, as though this island lifted, floated
In Indian baths . . .
—Hart Crane, "Island Quarry"

Contents

Acknowledgments

I am grateful to those journals where these poems first appeared, sometimes in earlier forms.

Alaska Quarterly Review: "The Gringo Called Ñakak"
Atlanta Review: "The Devil's Miner"
Callaloo: "Fetish"
The Caribbean Writer: "Village of the Water People" and "Elegy for Great-Uncle Julio, Cane Cutter"
The Cincinnati Review: "Golgotha" and *"Libros"*
Crab Orchard Review: "Sal" and "Aubade: The Charcoal Makers"
The Evansville Review: "Tantrums"
The Fiddlehead: "Panegyric for the Condor" and "Parable"
Huizache: "Den of the Lioness"
Image: "*El Cristo de Piedra*"
Indiana Review: "*Zafra*"
The Malahat Review: "Zvi Mendel"
New Letters: "Altiplano" and "Juancito's Wake"
PRISM *international:* "Mambo" and "*Refrigeradores*"
Shenandoah: "Ars Poetica" and "Mole"
Tar River Poetry: "Pyx" and "Adderall"
West Branch: "Courtyard of Clotheslines, Angel Hill"; "Tía Gladys, Backroom Seamstress"; and "Windfall Antiques"

I wish to express my deepest gratitude to the National Endowment for the Arts for a fellowship in 2009 that gave me the time off from teaching to complete this book. I also wish to thank the three judges of the Prairie Schooner Book Prize in Poetry

(Hilda Raz, Peggy Shumaker, and David St. John) who chose my manuscript out of hundreds submitted, and another heartfelt thanks to Kwame Dawes for believing in my work. I wish to acknowledge those poets who in the past years have given me encouragement and support, among them Michael Anania, Francisco Alarcón, Francisco Aragón, Rane Arroyo, Don Bogen, Richard Garcia, Maurice Kilwein Guevara, Pablo Medina, as well as my fellow writers at Notre Dame, and a very special thanks to Jacque Brogan for her insightful comments on the drafts for several poems in this collection.

Fetish

1. Ars Poetica

Ay, venga, paloma, venga
y cuénteme usted su pena.
—Nicolás Guillén, "Balada"

O come, dove, come
and tell me your sorrows.
"Ballad"

Courtyard of Clotheslines, Angel Hill

Though dark clouds hint the kind of rain
that strafes a city, the long drought has made
fresh water scarce as milk or gasoline.
Sand like raw sugar blows from Gabon,
burying creek and aqueduct alike,
even agaves wither in tin-can gardens,
and the women of Angel Hill make do
with shortages more numerous than bristles
on a pig. No meat today? They grind
plantain peels or pickle mop rags. No soap?
They churn clothes in boiled seawater,
rig sisal lines to iron balconies that crisscross
the stone courtyard like a cat's cradle,
and because Havana Bay is so close,
wayward gusts wreck the frazzled rope—
a darned diaper or threadbare blouse
tossed like some injured bird astray
in cumuli that scud Caribbean shores.
While clothes can be replaced by barter
or theft, those kin lost at sea are grieved
in shrines of patched photos, wild flowers,
the clay and cowrie-eyed Eleggua, "way opener,"
mollified by rum-soaked tobacco,
these desperate men and women, called *escoria*,
scum, by the government, who take

to the Florida Straits on rafts stitched
from boards, wire mesh, inner tubes,
whose hasty provisions fall overboard
in the high swells, who clamor to María
or Yemayá for sweet water, calm seas,
dry land, then plunge into the waves
when angels whisper from the brine.

Golgotha

In the Gospels a spare reference—
Gulgulta, Gulgoleth, Calvarium—
yet if etymology is just bedrock,
how, then, to visualize this place
of the skull? As a gnawed-out crag
of jaw impaling marrow skies,
adipose clouds? Or a knurled maw,
gargantuan granite, that mauls
the very sun but has never soaked
the volatile rain of Easter.

For his altarpiece at San Zeno
Mantegna paints a flattened knoll,
bald boulders, bilious horizon,
cobbles more decrepit than
gallstone, while Zurbarán
renders in chiaroscuro a pate
of clay, dried up, dun, and puny,
which even God Himself
would spurn to blow.

My Golgotha—*mi Gólgota*—
rose from Caribbean waters,
a karstic skull in a gully
of gauzed tobacco,
sprawling sugar cane,

flop-eared taro tufts,
my magnificent knob
of dog-toothed rock—
weed matted, bush mottled,
tree knotted, bog moated—
without lapsarian rubble,
without screes of sin,
without droughts
of dogma,
every calcite fissure
cragged
with *guayacán,*
evergreen that blooms
in the brine gales
of Lent, never blights
or burls, so dense
it sinks
like saints' bones
in seawater,
even the saltiest
Dead Sea,
whose embers
radiate haloes
in the darkest
Good Friday.

Fetish

Our Lady of Regla Church, Cuba

Beneath the sweetsop light
of stained glass, an Eleggua,
its head a smoked gourd carved with crosses
that sprout capillary roots,
inlays of cowrie shell
for eyes, nose, & mouth, a long tail
coiling into a rosary
of tamarind seeds.

Were guinea fowl sacrificed
among seagrapes on the breakwater?
Was goat's blood stirred
with molasses in coconut crania?
Who keeps vigil so the red
votive light does not die or ants
plunder the thimble of sugar?

Whoever laid you so near the altar
did not fear destruction.
Aren't priests supposed to crush
you with hobnailed heels
or the gentler sacristan sweep you out
to sea with a Palm Sunday broom?

Blessèd squatter, gorgeous stowaway
from the Bight of Benin,

I crave to take you home where snow
& hail fall from brittle clouds
that phosphoresce the night sky.
Don't fear. Snow is coconut flakes,
hail rock candy. I will paint
gouache jungles with aquatint vines,
ocher ceibas, orchids that grow
in gessoed moonlight, your lair
of Spanish moss by a bay window
where you will eat red papaya,
drink rum, sun like an iguana
on a *yagruma* tree.

Mambo

for Claude McKay

Old Habana's *catedral*: easterlight
bathes stone shrines in aquarelles of avocado,
papaya, and grapefruit, Our Lady's *retablo*,
hues of guava. From stained glass cages, birds take flight
as winged cherimoyas, bananas, and mangoes,
soar to tamarind skies. Censers of clove
burn to paschal ash; Carmelites tattoo the dove
with the lamb, quaff spirits, mambo in frescoes
of cane and banana. As ginger angels play
sweetsop güiros, coco *bongós*, the goat-skinned nuns
swirl on altars of sugar skulls, rummed tongues
trill conga canticles. Dance that ends with rays
of sunset muscovado, then dusk's scorched caramel,
till easterlight again fructifies to aquarelle.

Maracas of Rain

Grace is a coral island, Purgatory's Sea,
where penance is lax, shriving fun.
Want to flagellate? Sargasso abounds
to tickle your back, soft-shell crabs
for stigmatic cuts. Stomp your sins away
in the spume of tidal boleros,
wear a cotton-silk cilice to pray
on plush moss as breakers rumba
to thunder's timbale, maracas of rain.
Never a downburst or gale to rip
Christmas palms, just breezy vespers
for dozing on a hammock strung
between banana trees with bleeding hearts.
Sunny days to hobnob with angels
in the grotto, play saints'-bone dominoes,
enjoy acolytes' calypso, then at dusk
stroll down the nave of reliquary lamps
& songbirds in tabernacles. Mass is sumptuous
when passion buds bloom, the conch
stoups full of spicy rum, the Eucharistic cha-cha-cha
on brown-sugar sands, the moonlit vigil
for the roving Nazarene who'll glide down
a cliff of waves and surf you to rapture.

Aubade: The Charcoal Makers

inspired by the short Cuban film El Mégano (1955)

At sunrise when moths molt to orchids,
& moon frogs sleep in wetland hollows,
the peasants emerge from dead embers,
walking into daylight like bone marionettes
with charcoal skin, loincloths of bark.

Sunrays knife black water, a gust scythes
the wild cane, & men mine the muck, not gold
or agates, but fossil wood they pull out bare-
handed, heavy stumps that burn for days
in earthen mounds their children watch over,
tamping holes with black mud, flat stones.

If the oven does not overcook good wood
to cinder, the men canoe from palm hamlets,
sell their charcoal sacks to Don Ramón,
swamp's patrician, who pays with credit slips
that buy wet sugar, hard *bacalao*, old lard.
Don Ramón boasts he can eat three chickens
at a sitting, ramrod fists to make good on threats,

pistol packed in his waist, treating peasants
like milking goats, so docile, so dumb, he thinks,
when a woman smiles, waves as he glides

on his fancy boat, the beaming toddler who gives
a belly hug when offered some cadaverous
tuber to gnaw, something his Spanish hounds
would refuse, nor his prized gamecocks peck.

The revolution is coming, Don Ramón,
stealthy as gunpowder lit by red embers,
that day when peasants rise up at dawn,
burn down your domains in pitched skies,
ashen flurries like confetti, your daughters
drowned in the bog, your diamonds, your gold
fleeting as sugar & butter in a charcoal fire.

Zvi Mendel

Ersatz cantor, self-taught kabbalist,
retired tobacconist to Havana's Ashkenazim,
Zvi Mendel smokes one last corona
before the Sabbath, exhaling toward heaven,
strokes a tabby tom nipping green leaves
from Vuelta Abajo. Pigtails of maduro
festoon a sunny window, kewpie dolls wear
cigar-band crowns, & atop the cedar humidor
a wind-up gramophone wobbles *Für Elise.*

It's 1952, & though he's lived thirty years
on Calle Monte, his dead wife a pale goy,
a convert, from a cow town in Cienfuegos,
one son who married the maid, a cute
& salty girl, but—oy vey—black as coal tar,
another who turned communist & calls
the synagogue a pen of goats, Old Zvi won't
go completely native, mangling Spanish,
singing Torah on the tram, wearing wool
instead of linen, assailing the neighbors
in Yiddish when they party to *guarachas.*
Old Zvi eats only food canned in the U.S.—
kashrut beets, sauerkraut, corned beef—
says that Cuban meat is *traif*, the fish get
ciguatera from red tide, hens peck the swill,
even plantains ripen to a deathly funk.

But tobacco's the exception, Zvi argues,
if first grade, no mosaic, worms, or rust,
the drying done in barns clean of hogs.
Soaked in Seder wine, a plug becomes
incense, pipe's dottle is mourning ash,
& to prevent the evil eye, an amulet
of *picadura* strung around the neck.
Whether one inhales doesn't matter
because smoke, weightless, indigestible,
cannot be a defamation to YWHW.
How contemplation is not brought on
by knowing but by sucking a breva
or a panatela on a day when puffs
dance in the stale air of a sunlit room,
one cloud turning like a chariot wheel,
& Old Zvi in awe as the sparks of dust
arc into a tremulous rainbow, *shekinah*.

The Maximum Leader
Addresses His Island Nation

For half a century we have triumphed at war and insurrection, our legions victorious across the continents. The capitalist hordes succumb like ants to our Katyushas & Kalashnikovs. Our breath is napalm, our sweat nitroglycerin, our children's lullaby Fatherland or Death. Despite these martial glories, we are a poor island between the Tropics of Cancer and Capricorn. Winds betray us in the rainy season, droughts curse every nine years. Why should geography imprison us? I hereby decree that we are no longer tropical. Cut down the palms, my countrymen. Raze the mangroves. Uproot the papaya trees. Let barbwire brambles cover our valleys, steel conifers with grenades line our boulevards. After burning down the corn fields, dredging the rice sloughs, trampling every manioc hollow, you will sow rye with gunpowder, seed barley in bombshells. Because life is not a carnival but a wake of reason, you will not tell spicy jokes, play dominoes, or gyrate to drums. The polka will be our national dance, all food boiled and bland. Our homes will have fireplaces and no fans, windows sealed, verandas torn, parasols outlawed. You will wear wool coats and sheepskin boots, long johns, ear muffs too. Whoever faints or complains will be shot on sight. I will institute a ten-year plan in which every scientist and sorcerer will wage war on the tropics. Meanwhile you will walk through drifts of plastic snow, dry-ice cobbles, pretending to shiver, pretending that breath freezes in air, pretending that arctic winds crackle your face.

Spiderman in Havana

No claps, no cheers as Mary Jane kisses Spidey
upside down or when archfoe Green Goblin dies
impaled by his own glider. What made people rise
and holler in awe was the Butterball turkey
Aunt May sets on the Thanksgiving table, the load
of side dishes and yeast rolls sludged in butter,
and while such a succulent bird might not stir
Americans to noise, shouldn't the embargoed
Cubans have jeered or at least made some fuss
over the daily toil to appease a growling stomach?
Power hides in irony, the sly glee. To mock
one's suffering is the cleverest rage, a Tantalus
who smirks every time desire eludes his hand
or mouth, even as Sisyphus rolls his boulder
like some ox yoked to fate, the dumbest martyr
to a Cuban antihero—strategist in tricks, grand
swindler—who'd pimp Mary Jane, sow chaos
with the Goblin, amused by calamitous loss.

Den of the Lioness

An outcast since her release from political prison,
she lives on a rooftop next to a rain barrel,
raising chickens and growing tomatoes in cans
freckled with rust, her one-room house
built without screws or nails, a troweled gruel
of cement, sawdust, glass shards, the zinc roof
so hot gulls avoid it in the early afternoon.

As the journalist walks inside her door,
a small window glares like a Cyclops' eye.
Buenas tardes, he stutters, as if his tongue
had sprained. Her floor tilts when he sits
on a vinyl couch with jiggly chrome legs,
its honeycomb of holes fixed with wax.
Family photos in Styrofoam frames hang
from mildewed walls; a milk-bottle aquarium
rests on a table made from bowed planking.

Details get jotted hurriedly. He turns on
the tape recorder, and the woman tells stories
of teaching sharecroppers to read, write
in the cane fields of Villa Clara, her pride
wearing the militia's olive-green uniform,
how she broke a horse, slaughtered a pig,
thatched a hut. He cuts in, blurts *por favor,*
hand held up like a stop sign, says it's her

long imprisonment he's come to write about.
Readers want tragedy not happy pastorals.

She starts to weep, body crouching.
He flinches, then clutches her hand,
offering rum from his knapsack.
The rolling capstan continues to whirr
as she recalls those thirteen years
inside a cell the size of a broom closet,
a prison called Den of the Lioness,
where each day she ate boiled feed
dyed to look like grits, drank sewage
guards joked was chocolate milk,
tag-team beatings with electrical wire,

midnight firing squads that faked
her execution, harrowing hours
hung upside down from an empty well,
yet how despite all this suffering
she kept sane tending God's creatures
like St. Francis at Assisi, a lame rat
one night, a pregnant mouse another,
the croaking frog, the chirping cricket.

Libros

Hardbacks are the bricks
that prop a sinking
featherbed, while ragpaper
science fiction stows
away in a Soviet fridge
shorted by blackouts.
As novellas sprawl on
a sailcloth loveseat,
hemp-bound histories
spiral in corners spackled
with lard and sawdust.
Termites are mulchers
of monographs, molds
colonize the sun-crackled
tome, house mice nest
in the scrunched tracts
of Marx and Engels.
During thunderstorms
gusts scatter pages
beyond wood windows,
beyond iron balconies,
flock of a thousand
that flaps over hills,
glides past breakwaters,
then falls—feathered—
into pulping waters.

Refrigeradores

Our genius *el invento*, the quick, jury-rigged fix,
we bring back to life geriatric iceboxes—
pre-Castro GE's, Frigidaires, Westinghouses—
with scavenged parts, filched spares, junked thingamajigs.
Even the ancient monitor-top gets an overhaul—
a moped's two-stroke, Czech-made, crammed inside
the fridge's cowl; two peg legs; the large latch pried
from a dead Soviet truck. Bolted to an outside wall,
a car-plate windmill pumps freon to a Kelvinator,
while door hinges, a barrel bolt resurrect the rusted-out
Philco. Caulked cassava starch, thick as grout,
plugs a Cold Spot, incontinent in the night,
though the Dodderer can still freeze a guinea hen.
Praise be to the fixer, the handyman, the *juan-*
of-all-trades, our wily tinkerer, troubleshooter on
the fly, more useful than doctor or politician,
whom necessity has made scrounger, thief, cannibal,
who makes miracles with dogged craft, the found tool.

Elegy for Great-Uncle Julio, Cane Cutter

Martí Sugar Mill, Matanzas, Cuba, 1998

Growing up in Miami I never heard his name,
my aunts hissing *comunista*, his image cut
from photos, his letters torn. "Fool, let him eat swill
in paradise," Uncle Manny would say as he
bit ripe tomatoes like apples, dimple dripping.

I wait in darkness, sitting on an oxhide chair,
smell of sinew, tallow. Tío Julio's *bohío*,
palm thatched, tobacco leaves like animal skins
nailed to walls of peeled bark; cradled by a rag
doll, the radio gargles sugar-harvest statistics.

Wakened from his nap, Tío Julio shuffles
on *bagasso* slippers, sputters when I say
I'm Cuca's grandson, sister he hasn't seen since
New Year's '59, day a triumphant Fidel
entered La Habana like Hannibal on a Sherman tank.
Cowrie shells augured exile. Few listened.

Knees buckle, fingers claw my wrist.
I lay him on a mattress stained by urine,
wilted clippings of Fidel glued to bedposts.
Stroke scarred hands, arms as if touch
could heal a lifetime cutting cane in the sun.

Tío's wife rejoices when I give her fat pork
bought from a butcher pushing a broken bicycle,
pig guts like eels in brine. Brings *cafecito*,
chicory coffee, tepid, bilgy water, raspy dregs.
I swallow to be polite. Opening a cigar box,
he shows me freckled photos of ancestors:

men who tilled with wood plows, slow oxen
fields that withered early in the planting season,
arroyos and ditches evaporating to molasses.
One sepia print shows a girl switching a mule,
Cuca at twelve, looking stern because teeth
had grown crooked on the cobs. Voice crackles

when I promise to tell Abuela how ill he is,
that his nieces will write soon. "Politics
should never divide family," Amelia says,
and I give her $20, press the bill into her hand.
"So soon, stay for dinner." "*No puedo*," I say,
fib that the last mill-train leaves at dusk.

Tall as royal palms, smokestacks spew ghosts
of the sugar harvest; dismembered,
Soviet tractors rot in sheds, corrugated tin.
Boys playing baseball chase me across
the yuca thickets. *Cuoras, chocolate, chicle,*

they plead, hurling rocks when I say no.
On these rutted canefields I trip over pits
of memory, red dust stinging my eyes,
I the bearer of dollars, false promises.

Tía Gladys, Backroom Seamstress

Garments crowd on the rack, overrun their boxes
As Tía, clocked, threads fast, pedals, runs the feed dogs
To stretch waists, sew buttons, hem cuffs, seam crotches—
Tensile loops, rivet-tight knots, a conga of cogs
In lockstitch. While no *modiste* at sprucing hand-me-downs,
Thrift-store orphans, Tía watches Lawrence Welk
To learn fashion, draws on paper bags bridal gowns
That whirl, silk skirts like tourniquets, talks of a boutique
For barrio girls who aspire to clothes with corselette.
One day she plays *la bolita*, & though winning small,
Tía waltzes with bubbles. By week's end she quits
Work, gets a rush loan, her Dodge Dart, collateral.
Tricks out her room like a shop, buys tulle, satin bolts.
Knocks door to door: cash orders, layaway dreams.
Sews days & night, grows thin, pale as lace. Girls revolt
Over bad fits, nail-breaking buttons, skewed seams.
Business dead, she rides the bus, works for less, her trust,
Her faith unbroken, even when luck goes bust.

Zafra

Province of Matanzas, Cuba, 1919

Season of sugar harvests, saint's day sweethearts:
One-legged François trundles on a donkey cart
Across the rutted roads of mill towns to shoot
Plump brides in starched flax, silk sashes, calfskin boots,
Whose gaunt fathers would plow granite to pay
Dowries, trousseaus, sacristy fees. Night and day
Steam trains freight hogshead molasses, crates of rum,
Sugar gems, at first dirty and blotched, then spun
First water for traders in London, Vienna, Brussels.
Though Europe's in ruins, sharecroppers shuffle
To maracas, three-string guitars, drink the green
Cane juice, the price of sugar highest it's ever been,
Till the market steepens, saturates, succumbs
To traders' glut and soon free-falls like Icarus.

But on this feast of St. Jude, boys romp in the cane
Fields, torching hives of weed, laying down ratsbane,
Slingshooting buzzards that linger for carrion,
While sisters betrothed at twelve fumble rumpled gowns
And primp with cascarilla, coal dust, marrow grease,
Twirl crooked parasols, furl moth-eaten fans as they wheeze
In corsets to pose on rawhide, a screen of cheesecloth.
Most girls would have flirted with the hooded box,
But Grandma Cuca—gelder, cane cutter, roughrider—

Scowls, squirms, silt of makeup cracking, who'd spur
Broncos bareback than sit sidesaddle in the sun.
Wedding bells peal, her eyes sting, throat burns. "Nun
Or whore," she thinks, "you're still a branded mare,"
And seethes with white satin cinched to a snare.

Ars Poetica

After an oiled stone whet the chinked blade,
Papá planed leftover lumber, groomed the grain
With emery rags, nipped shards, buffed to suede
Every nick and scratch then smeared an oily stain;
Armoire, cupboard, credenza, or stool, each made
To outlast mold's caprice, rot's relentless reign—
A cement shed, pawnshop tools, Papá got paid
With cardboard IOU's but didn't complain,
Dallied bills, snubbed calls, worried about dirt
Spoiling beeswax, a runny varnish, the hair
That strayed into seamless shellac, while I gave
Succor to fractures, restored scraps, healed the wart
On a lacquered pine leg, vigilant in my care
Of salvaged wood as it bucked the austere lathe.

2. El Cristo de Piedra

Odysseus: So you pick up various stories and you stitch them?
Demodocus: The sea speaks the same language around the
world's shores.
—Derek Walcott, *The Odyssey: A Stage Version*

Windfall Antiques

Overdrawn, repoed Grand Prix, workshop in hock
To the dogs, Papá mends houses of refugees
Who niggle over how much grout to squeeze
Into a crack, who bathe in their girdles and socks
To skimp on Fab. Checks bounce, taxmen hound, the truck's
Muffler shot, Papá scouts groomed lawns for settees,
Divans, chaises meant for Goodwill, windfall antiques
To fix with mallet, strainer, needle, twine, & chalk.
"Waste is for gringos," he'd say, tapping brass nails
That wiggle on warped pine or straining buckram
On a crippled carcass, my hands dull as I shear
Chintz for skirts, though Papá, reverent with details,
Irons burlap, measures the tweed sleeves & trim
In metrics, smoothes out horsehairs to cashmere.

Horses

Miami Military Academy, 1972

Wee hours, hard rain, our shower pit
trenched from horse graves, the old stable
scuttled into the murk of Biscayne Bay;
we totter on a lattice of naked boys, our ears
pressed against the leaky showerheads
eager for brass whinnies or a drain's squeal.
Beneath a row of sinks, Jim Lewin sobs,
lips torn, ballooned nose, this night
the first he's lost a fistfight to a plebe.
Though he lisps like Daffy Duck, & his belly
drizzles lard as it bounces in the sun,
Lewin stomps our feet with a rifle's butt
but worse is the wire hanger he shoots
like a crossbow as we curl in shackled cots,
piled blankets our only shields. Boys
who lie bare incur nicks, bleeds, the poked eye;
I hide inside lockers, scrounge rinds
of smuggled bread, haunt the hallways
in soiled skivvies, bug sores around
the groin I soothe with saddle soap. One night
after snorting buckles' Brasso dust,
smoking banana peels, I yank Lewin
from the top bunk, & with eyes taut,
teeth vising tongue, I pelt, kick, scratch
till belly fat bloats the nails' quick,

then trot, rear, reel out Spanish curses.
Sweat cools like alcohol when wind
scampers through the barracks, & I hear horses
trampling through the treeless grounds,
hooves that rip concrete as if silt of rivers.

Lalo, Peddler

Rainy shoes squeaking like a dog's toy, his hat (or was
it a piked helmet?) of papier-mâché, sticks, & gauze,
he'd slosh into my uncle's plumbing store to peddle
oranges, coconut sweets, fried dough, sticky balls
of sesame called angels' lice, his slung box
nailed from scrap wood, crumpled tin, rubber blocks.
Tangelos in bright bags swung from his belt,
sometimes tipping over loose porcelain or gaskets
in a tray, which made plumbers laugh & Uncle
Manny call him a dwarf because of his small
legs, huge head, yet he was more like a compact
bull who could out-bellow a passing diesel truck.
When plumbers haggled over pennies just to tease,
he'd smile with gapped dentures, still happy to please
anyone praising his peeler, a Gillette-blade gadget
he'd rigged with odd parts from the flea market.

I was thirteen, my first summer threading steel pipe,
cutting cast iron, stacking toilets, enduring snipes
from ditch-digging plumbers who belched beer, drooled rum,
peed on me; I so hated them I'd pray for a magnum,
blow brains to marmalade. Once, Lalo saw me wedged
between PVC crates where I'd gone to sulk, cringe,
& he bear-hugged so hard I felt a burning clot
down my throat, cold shivers, my knees in a knot.
Lalo's hands, rinds of callus, yanked me like a stump,

loaded me with tangelos, then we slumped
into the downpour, stumbling over puddles, hawking
to outdo thunder, jet planes overhead, the ping
of a pick-up truck on northwest seventh street
where exiles bought houses decaying in the heat,
the rain, abandoned by white flight, & set up
dime stores, bodegas, necessity's pawn shop.

Television, a Patient Teacher

Never a nag, mean word, our color Quasar in the sunroom
where Mr. Rogers purled droplets of praise, and I could forget
the clang of Miss Dorn's burro bell when I said *shadow*
like *chado*, stretched the O's of wood and good into a U.
Mamá's gleaming bathroom, a language lab, where I stood
before the gold mirror to chew in Cronkite monotones,
pop like bazooka gum those plosive *P*'s, *B*'s that pummeled
Batman's foes. After a hot bath, I'd practice the tidal schwas
of Captain Kangaroo, my vaporous face breaking up,
drips and streaks on cold glass, the mouth swollen, rubbery,
a cephalopod in eddies. Within three years, I could pass
for a Hoosier or a Buckeye, Mamá proud I'd mastered a tongue
that to her sounded like a sick dog. *El castellano* retreated
into memory, dreams, the once proud hidalgo humbled
to chatter. No quitter, it began to lurk, mind's liminal wilds,
borderlands between the conscious and unconscious,
a *guerrillero*, a trickster, resisting English, his usurper.
As in a game of musical chairs, El Padre Nuestro lost
his throne to the Lord's Prayer, but any requests, my talk
with God, in sovereign *castizo*. To break writer's block,
think like a child, I free-write *en español*, squelching any intrusions
by Lord English. After an argument with my wife,
those words I regret are hard nasals, caustic fricatives,
but *cariñito* cloys like guayaba paste on a sticky afternoon.
Colleagues call me *cubano*, rounding out vowels like smoke,
which pleases me enough to wear *guayabera*, pestle cumin
with garlic, fix saints to the dash, let rice boil over the pot.

Sal

When butter burns I remember sundowns
of grilled cheese sandwiches, newspaper doilies;
corn chips gone soggy, larders in the rain,

Sal's grandmother's kitchen, a greenhouse
where wire-caged orchids—wild pines, *Epidendrums*—
dangled from broken windows, centipede vines

crept cupboards gemmed with taffy-glass snails,
cerulean whorls. Hot days asphalt smoked like grease,
Granny Mae ladled grape Kool-Aid from a hog pail,

smothered *sweetie pies, honey chiles* in molasses,
chuckled when I said beach as bitch, dessert as desert,
that *frito-bandito* talk Miss Jones called *uglier than*

spit on dirt: I, the only Spanish boy in Goulds,
swamp dredged for ranch homes, groves of alligator
pear, La Sagüesera, Cuban town, a world away.

The year astronauts first walked on the moon
Sal was my sole friend, the one who pelted bullies,
square-dance partner when others kicked me

in the knees. Sal too an outcast: orphan girl,
poorest in sixth grade, fat tomboy with dark skin,
quarter Seminole, grandmother's shotgun

shack across weedy railroad tracks. Pockets
squishy with baitworms, we rode to brackish sink-
holes, glass-sharp limestone, brittle as eggshells;

cast cardboard reels to hook spotted gar, bluegills,
swallowed gummy flesh with Diablo sauce, braided guts
into necklaces, played stickball with heads. Nightfall,

we climbed gumbo-limbos to slurp bromeliad
water, dead leaves roosting like bats, fingerbone twigs;
trudged sloughs where bullfrogs bubbled in mud

wombs, food for pet indigos, scarlet kingsnakes.
Sometimes hot air gusted from faraway sawgrass fires,
wilting leaftips, mossbuds, & hundreds of gambusia

would leap like sparks, oölite ponds, gulping fig
crickets, fly larvae—the water milky, tart, almost scalding.
We belly-flopped holding hands, her tiny teeth—

burrs of bone—nibbled lobes, cock's-spur toes
scratched shins raw. *You're mine now,* Sal said, *I the boy,*
you the girl. Beneath dwarf liana vines, she painted

my lips red acacia, drew circles around nipples,
made a wig from Spanish moss. I tucked genitals between
legs, tiptoed in *tacones,* Mamá's stiletto heels;

she bit puckered *labios,* slug tongues rubbing together,
our bed wet humus, moldy naseberry *flores. This is how*
it's done, Sal said, arms taut, spine arched, her seesaw

motion *un cachumbambé,* throat gurgling spring-
rain *bambú,* fluttering eyes, *zunzún* wings. Wind singed
tender parts of orchids—stigmas, anthers, ovaries—

I felt my arms crawl through the undergrowth,
ficus roots—*jagüey*—that climbed high canopy of *caoba,*
sapote, wild *tamarindo,* seed pods sticky as geckos;

neck stretched out into the sea, aigrette fronds
growing from my head, speckled petioles of palm;
legs dug into peat, snaked miles through aquifer,

toes sprouting low tide as mangrove breathing tubes,
soft-mud *manglar negro.* Through galled ears, saltwater oak,
I heard *corúa* birds coo the dawn *gru-gru, gru-gru.*

Village of the
Water People

Pinar del Río Province, Western Cuba

Withers sore, splinted cannons, our horses balk,
whinny as they clamber the slippery summit
where coconut trees cleave diorite and ficus vines

snarl the heliconia. Huddled over karstic crags
are small houses with green eaves and terracotta tile,
the day's wash strung between dead lemon trees.

A hen chases wind-blown corn, ants smother a piglet,
a bony donkey forages in the shade of a broken outhouse.
Tented with old cheesecloth, seedlings grow in cots

of manure, gourds proliferate along serpentine ledges,
bougainvilleas take root in ammonite. I almost fall
when my horse races to water, trampling across boxes

used for raking coffee beans like scorched beetles.
A lean, older woman named Marilú, wearing a gown
of rags, crown of weeds, hemp sandals, welcomes us

with grassy coffee, coconut cakes, juicy mango slices.
Her round eyes are charcoal, her coarse hair in long braids
like banyan roots. My guide Beto, a farmer who rents

spare horses to tourists, grins with a full mouth. I eat too,
though woozy. It's overcast, almost five, yet sunlight
flares through a crack in the clouds; her thin fingers

flutter as she takes my donation. We go inside a dirt-
floor hut with shiny calabash cups on a long table
like a raft of sticks and stalks; clay saints fill the holes

of a shallow outcrop where knobby candles burn and water,
limy and warm, seeps from a green gash. Our Lady
sighs in lithographs pinned with thorns to palm-leaf walls.

Marilú explains this is where they drink each day to keep
health, cure disease, pray to Mary, a doxology or a rosary, in sips
and slurps. No rush, no quaffs, she says, let the taste linger,

then grasps my hand, shows me how, so hard the gourd
just about cracks, and a buttery warmth fills my esophagus,
belly growling from the confluence of water and acid.

The hut grows dark, but I can hear whispers, or is it crickets,
toads? A horse neighs, maybe two, then a quick gallop
that makes the ground shudder. I worry that Beto has left

just as it starts to rain. Marilú takes me to a bed of pink
blossoms, pillowed leaves; we drink from the same calabash.
Our legs cross, her varicose veins like fissures in a rock.

Her hands touch my face, numbing skin, mouth. I mumble
with limestone lips, gritty throat. I'm a believer, she says,
but just don't know it. My image in the cup told her secrets.

Submit, be reverent, she says, and feel the grace of wet earth
on your feet, rain's tingling mercy on your skin. Strong arms
carry me outside, drop me on gravel. The water people hold hands,

pray in a circle, drink from the sky. Rattan reliquaries
glow with fireflies. I take small, soggy steps, join the circle,
sit in a puddle, hum a hymn, spider lilies in the wind.

El Cristo de Piedra

Valle de Viñales, Cuba, 2002

In this valley where limestone hills jut out
like hairy moles over furrows of tobacco,
a rock-face Christ sprawls on a skew cross,
as if a child had taken loose chert to etch
his fanged mouth, stick legs, twigged fingers.

I touch gouged eyes that weep candle wax,
caress his ocher heart, pray to have a child—
five years of dud pills, junk shots, toxic teas,
specialists who insist, *your wife's plumbing works,*
her hours clocked to Clomid, Cetrotide, hCG,
fridge a mosaic of Rx's, labs, medals, holy cards.

I scratch the ground for a sign: a root gnarled
like a crucifix, a seashell Mary, fig leaf's scapular,
but only dig up a few termites dried to husk.

By year's end we adopt a Panamanian girl,
certain that Ivis would not conceive. Around
March she gets fits of heartburn, thinks it's
acid reflux, then faints, vomits one morning.
Doctor orders a blood test. Days later Ivis calls
me at work with the good news, I in a daze,
her mother in Miami sure that her long-distance

novenas had worked, if late. God's miracle?
Or was it vagrant chance that made the play?
Either way, faith is deep water that wears away
the rocks of reason, washes out silt of creed,
unstable, profligate, resistant to doubt's gravity.

Birthing Adrian

All bruised up as if hit by a truck going ninety,
Baby's head round, stony, a bowling ball
I had to get out, squeeze this bone brute free,
Don't let it jam my insides, a cannon's stopple;
How cold the room, a fog of sweat, time's speed
A relief, or was it the epidural, the iv's feed
Of Pitocin? Then the lump was gone, purple
Bundle with wails, and you cut the cord after all
Your snores through labor, having to elbow you awake.
Hated too how I had to push out the afterbirth,
Not sheer, silky, an awful blob, like offal, to avert
One's gaze. But holding our baby I could make
Out his pug nose, puckered mouth, thrilled he was intact,
Alive, no sonogram blur, fetus brooding in a sac.

Tantrums

Combustive, fickle as nitro, a toddler's temper
Detonates to hunger's fuse, a whim's tripwire.
Boredom ignites airbursts, headbangs, the crier
Prone to napalm meltdowns at mall or 4-H fair.
When my son has a fit I hear the dentist's drill
Boring out bone, steel fingernails' glissando
On a chalkboard, those high-voltage shrieks, O-
Scope shock waves, my ears pinging like anvils—
Teeth gnashing, jaw spasms that yoga breaths fail
To soothe. Soon my toes curl up, that fling
Of rage with trembles, my nerves flayed raw.
I stop, saved by the angel of guilt. Love's not frail
But tensile, resistant to grudges, set to spring
As I hush, dance him in my arms, bent to his law.

Braille

Panamá, 2002

The broken cab hobbles out the airport, potholes big
as wash tubs. A bolt pops out. I hold the strap tight.
No second thoughts. Once the consular paperwork
is done, Valerie, three years old, newly parented, will fly
to America with a green card, patent leather shoes.
I break a sweat. Crack open the duct-taped window.
Wind's hiss, colicky, irks my nerves. Everywhere I look
cement houses, unfinished husks, like playpens

at an orphanage. *Let's get this done fast,* my wife
says on the phone, our cash short, one card maxed out—
a Sony laptop with WiFi and video for the judge
to release her ward. Call it a donation. Call it a bribe.
I don't care. Ivis won't leave empty-handed.
Cured every mite, amoeba, louse. Bought a dozen
Barbies, Cinderella slippers, a carousel of gowns.
Close to the hotel, fears ricochet. Will the child sense

my doubts? She's too restless even for a toddler,
bouncing, grabbing anything within reach.
It worries me she won't fall asleep, shaking the crib slats,
flipping over the rails, a sofa's barricade. X-rays
show a plate above the left temple, non-metal, like a patch
on a pair of jeans. Doctor's verdict: good blood flow,
no nerve damage, seamless fusion, the skull fractured
at eight months by her mother, a deported *dominicana*

dragging her suitcase of shame, or did she pack light,
a keepsake lock, those baby photos she meant to frame,
regrets like spare change in a Gerber jar? Let judges judge.
I brood over blood, her genes' bequeathal, every cell
a Pandora's box. Take a chance, trust in fate,
I say, as we enter the city center, Vía España, a hive
of scabbed cars, belching buses, hawkers. The cab stops
at the hotel, honks for bellboys playing marbles.

Fighting sleep, my feet heavy, I walk into the room,
Valerie in Dora jammies, pink slippers. Her small hands
do not fumble or paw in the faint light but linger over
my face as if bumps, bristles, and pits were Braille.
I wince hearing *Papá* as she clings to my neck, pulls hair,
climbs a bent knee. I give her a long hug, loud kiss
on the cheek, my hand touching an ear, tracing the soft
jawline, her brown eyes bright on a July morning.

Pyx

Grotto of Our Lady of Lourdes, Notre Dame, Indiana

Wrought cross, wounds of rust; ice-welted saints; a rosary
That thaws in a bronze bowl, pyx of pleas. Valerie,
Giggling, snags it, a new necklace. Crows caw, flap low,
Silty clouds, specks of rain. She runs into the grotto,
Afraid of loud birds, thunder too, but will do handstands,
Cartwheels in a snowstorm. Beware to forget her pill—
She'll eat pencils, cut clothes, glue lips, staple ears at school.
We feed the money box, light candles, kneel in spring air.
Mother of God, help me not break things, be good, not litter,
She prays, her crossing astray. I correct cold hands,
But she twists in my arms, darts toward the lakeside park.
Afraid she'll get hit by a car, I chase, skies now dark,
& scold. She cries, kicks, but piggyback can console.
She plucks her beads; I drop a wrung plea in the bowl.

Adderall

Each morning she takes the capsule, plump, buoyant
Like a pod in gastric swells, swift to grant a lull,
Bring peace, our girl released from chaos, pliant
To tasks, no screech, no bites, as beads of Adderall
Cast off, implant in neurons, sprout molecular
Edens that bloom till twilight when they start to wilt,
Dying before bedtime, the brain clamorous for
Gardens to be resown on fallows of synaptic silt.
I hear zealots: disorder's divine, needs no cure.
Bless flaws, yield to nature's draw. And forfeit too
Insulin if needed? I drop guilt's garment, sure
I've made the wiser choice. Open your eyes:
Watch Valerie make sunrays with candy foil, glue
Castles from wood scraps, swirl sand to butterflies.

St. Joseph River

Compared to the Amazon, an overgrown brook,
Servile to industry, timid flooder, flows that skein
In shimmers, river that zigzags the shale plain
Like my late aunt's blind stitching when she took
Cognac for cramps. Downtown, a sharp crook
North toward the lake, weathered docks, the bane
Of gutted factories, boarded storefronts, that eyestrain
I get driving on rust-belt roads that overlook
The coal-gray drifts, an occasional floater gored
By willow tusks, the last oak leaves taking flight, spun
In gusts, their tumultuous glide on lathing eddies,
Sawtooth ripples that portend more snow, the sword
Of ice rusting out iron piles, bridge where Adrian,
My son, fed the geese, then one day slid as if on skis,
Spring's blustery sprees,
Yet I quick enough, Thank God, to catch him before
The plank's edge. Late by one second, would tragedy's door
Have burst open, the floor
Of normalcy caving? Job would laugh at such a thing,
Like moths we hover over chaos, our lifeline a silk string.

Ashes

Valerie veers off to chase the pebbled snowdrift,
A March afternoon when the oaks should have shed
Their icicles. Downwind, I run Jingles to the vet,
Eyes marbled, bloody towel, & leap the pavement's rift,
A weft of dry branches, my wife struggling to lift
Adrian stuck in a hole. Too late, our old dog dead,
Nature's course, Vet says, cannula poking the spread
Of large warts. I pay for ashes to be sown, sift
Through forms to sign, leave with a tap on the rump.
Tears ice, breath frosts, but BK's near. We cross through
Frozen slush, kids pestering for chicken, a prize
Of crayons. Valerie draws Jingles in heaven. A plump
God sits on a throne. Hot dogs to eat, pig ears to chew,
Bacon bits that flurry from mashed-potato skies.

Mole

Soot spews as I mow the knee-high grass cobwebbed
With dew. Clogged blades, slicked feet, I heave up the knoll
Of weeds till the mower chokes, sneezes gas, then roll
It sideways, gut out the cuds, & squeezing the dead
Man's switch, I crank, gun, vroom the sod. Overhead
Clouds quilt charcoal skies, thunder gurgles. Ivis strolls
To the boombox, spins salsa, comes back to poke holes
With the neighbor's dibble. *Más bulbos* for our bed
Of tulips, she shouts. I cut the engine, trudge mud
To the garage. Gusts quake the maples, limbs crack—
Our squatter scats, squeaks, breaks for the solace
Of crates. I shriek the news; she nags, my trap's a dud,
Commands, *Mátalo ya*, & I push, jab, split, whack
With oak, then inter the mole with the bulbs of Ivis.

3. The Gringo Called Ñakak

Las piedras no ofenden; nada
codician. Tan sólo piden.
amor a todos, y piden
amor aun a la Nada.
—César Vallejo, "Las piedras"

Stones do not offend; nothing
do they covet. They just ask
to love everyone; they even ask
to love Nothingness.
"Stones"

Soroche

Peruvian Andes, 1985

At thirteen thousand feet, high enough to skydive,
legs turn to lead as I lurch down a crumpled road
above Lake Titicaca, heaving from hypoxia, every brain cell
a firecracker, signs of *soroche*, mountain sickness.

Bad dreams make me jump from bed, hit the door
with Shining Path graffiti, my paperboard room
in a mud-brick pensión, bare-wire bulbs, a wood stove
where a Quechua woman makes me coca tea—

scant relief. The more I moan; the more she scolds,
chew the leaves. I refuse. Will I turn into a junkie?
But Scottish Glen, five years trekking the altiplano,
Nods to say his lungs now sponge the thin air
like an Andean plowman's, his ramshackle teeth

mossy from all the coca in his rag satchel. To save
on lodging, redhead Glen sleeps on the kitchen floor,
wears alpaca weaves and rope sandals, his fingers
smelling of guinea pig roasted in sulfurous spices.
Glen torments me with stories of dead tourists—

embolisms, edemas, aortas bursting like brake lines,
the dusky cyanosis and paradoxical bradycardia.
Third day, I get sicker with ataxia, dizziness,
ask Glen to take me to a pharmacy or a red-cross clinic

but instead lugs me to the market where women
in derby hats squat behind hillocks of crackly coca,
cheek-wads like cue balls. Glen buys enough
to tip the copper scale, puts some inside my mouth,
ash too, says don't chew but let it steep awhile,
then suck the grainy juice, nauseatingly bitter,
causing a slight gag as the saliva starts to well up.

Within minutes I get a sugary rush, a tickle
in my crotch, a tittering bolt through my calvarium,
a soft weightlessness in the legs. By this time
he's already chugged a pitcher of corn beer,
and as I watch Glen dance with another drunk,

a plowman pretending to play a *quena* flute,
eyes red, his fingering jumbled, short legs smooth
with mud, I wonder if the conquistadores,
a mere thirteen dozen, were buzzed on coca
as they hacked to victory, an empire's fate
decided by a narcotic, not divine intervention.

The Gringo Called Ñakak

Based on Quechua folklore

White is the color of chalk. White is the sap from a rubber tree. I am translucent, just a faint shimmer, as I prowl your potato fields in the cold air, night turning to day, like soft ripples in a thawing brook. You might hear my feet crack an ice puddle, but you're too slow for my flying poncho. My elastic mouth will swallow your child if she strays into the willows or the eucalyptus grove. These blue eyes, brighter than a cat's, harder than gemstone, can track you in a moonless night. Don't hide in a cave, behind a boulder, or among the haystacks. I can sense your heat from a footprint, a sigh, your arms as they brush against the maize. Get me mad, and I'll breathe fire hot enough to boil a whole glacier to steam. I can grind your bones to powder with my diamond teeth, then sell it to druggists in China who'll make pills, elixirs, unguents. My fingernails are scalpels that harvest eyes, kidneys, and hearts for whoever pays the most in dollars, Euros, or British pounds. I own your mountains, from dry foothill to snowy peak. Like sentinels atop the cordillera, smokestacks soar into glass-wool clouds, and my cauldrons of steel produce lucrative lubricants. Night and day, sleet or hail, they refine the vacuumed fat of those I kidnap, those I buy, those I trick, your neighbor, your wife's cousin, your own daughter. Without them global progress would cease. Engines would die, guns would not fire, lasers would go dim, even satellites would fail to orbit the earth.

Altiplano

Priest's collar, black fedora,
dreamseller sits behind a desk lifted by sacks
of sand, his customer a highland woman
with cable braids, pom-pom hat like a lampshade.

Stolid, no tears, *la serrana* confesses
barrenness, not even stillborns
drowned in womb's sea. *I'm dry
like the puna, no curandera can cure me,*
she says, her man shacking in town
with *una mestiza, fertile like a sow.*

It's Easter, rocks glint violet light,
clouds glide toward the Pacific, reborn as foam.
If Christ can rise from the dead,
dreamseller declares,*"anything is possible*

if you pray with faith. Slapping his Remington
when it stutters the *P* in Perú, he types
the birth certificate—boy named Jesús María
for good luck—signs with pencil stump,
rubber stamp worn out like old gums.

On a barren hill men play with Tonka
look-alikes, letterpressed titles in shirt pockets,
dreaming dump trucks they hope will bring meat
each day, a house that stays dry in the cold rain;

wives build houses from scattered stones,
deeds glued to craggy facades, corn-beer blessings.

For ten *soles*, laborer's daily wage,
la serrana buys a rag doll, green yarn
for swaddling bands, a llama rattle.
Spins Wheel of Saints, arrow pointing
to Santa María, called *Pacha Mama*—
Mother Earth—since Inca times.
Offer chicha at sunrise, dreamseller says,
sacrifice a snow-white llama.

Cuddling her doll, she descends icy
cerros the following day, down paths
hooves, feet have eroded into rivulets

of devotion; the outcrop shrine is carved
with angels, half-human, half-animal.
She makes libations, drapes the plumed
granite cross with young llama skins.

Peaks tremble, the condor-headed archangel
breaks out of sacred rock. *It's God's will;
you shall have your son*, he says: guts out sawdust,
stuffs rag doll with Holy Ghost's viscera,

smears blood on eyes and mouth, slaps buttocks.
La serrana signs the cross when she hears
birth cries, but these turn to squawks as the doll
sprouts rainbow feathers, horned toes, beak,
and the ragbird flies toward the sun, riding updrafts,
disappearing into the blue phosphorescence.

Panegyric for the Condor

O Vulture that hovers andesite peaks & glacial
Gullies raising broods in the black-ice spurs
Of granite ledges, while Mama Killa, Mother Moon,
Rolls down to sleep in her hammock of hematite.
Your obsidian wings, ten-foot span, slice the mesh
Of mist, glide through night's hailing spar.
Your eyes, ocher or cinnabar, keen for blessings
Of carrion by a frozen lake or those craggy slopes
Guanacos climb to graze *tola* shrub, *ichu* grass.
Messenger Apu Kuntur who crosses the world
Of the righteous dead—Hanan Pacha—to hiss
A chant in fashion, carry gossip on quipu strings.
Majestic soarer of thermals in tungsten twilights
When clouds fray to silver dross & the cold rain
Drops as beads of mercury, winter's rosary.

The Devil's Miner

Potosí, Bolivia

The mountain eats men alive by forty-six.
Silicosis. Tuberculosis. A kid's
Life shorter: cave-ins, gas, dynamite.
Coca makes me strong to crawl through veins white
With arsenic, dig out innards for the fat
Of her silver, tend to the smelter's acid vat.
Wages belong to Mamá but Christmas season
I sneak to the market down the mountain,
Buy my younger siblings, who call me Papi,
Toys, paper, cotton candy. School clothes for me.
Going to class is like vacation from the mine.
Sundays we pray, sing psalms, get in line
For the Host. Yet God cannot reach deep inside
The mine, so there we praise the devil, abide
Tío's tastes, whims, with whiskey, a newborn
Goat, coca leaves. His clay horns, tongue's thorns,
Blood eyes scared me at first, but I struck a bargain.
Keep me alive & your star will brand my skin.
Now we're friends who smoke, laugh by torch light.
Never offend Tío. You'll die before night.

The Boy from Chimbote

In this coastal city beset by fish meal
Factories, scams, pickpockets who cop a feel,
I met two Quebecers at the youth hostel,
Playing cards before lunch, Pierre & Margot
Who hitched on trucks, mules, a steamboat
With bananas, goats. Street kids in tow,
We jostled to a vegan shack praised by Routard,
Slung packs to poles, ordered the starred
Cau Cau for lunch. Before we could ward
Him off, a curly teen plopped on a beanbag,
shook hands, gleam of gold teeth, a silk U.S. flag
Lassoing his neck. He prattled English, a gag,
It seemed, with disco beat, Motown shout,
Parroting our words and gestures, the bout
Of laughter, shrugged when I tried to out
Him with cuts, stabs of Castilian invective.
When peddlers approached us, he'd give
Nods, winks, quick pantomimes, the riff
Of gibberish, as if cast in a play by Genet.
Pierre blew up, hurled a spoon, the boy's bray
Horrendous. Nervous, I offered to pay,
Glad to leave on the next bus. Margot took
A liking to him, though, hugged that skinny crook
Of his long arms, taught the boy to look,
Talk French, who gurgled at her purse mirror,
Flounced to ballet, pouted an operatic air,
A diva sashaying by the Seine's shore.

Parable

Don Rey commands *peones* to hedge his chalet
With barbwire, graft floodlights, the hovels' creek
Poisoned with arsenic, and though these bleak
Foothills are goldless, the poor do not stray
Far from his cistern, his carob trees, his corn bin,
But glean only rats to boil in onion broth, eke
Marrow from stingy bones. Wind's sigh or creak
Of wood riles Don Rey to gun down any glint,
Stalk any shudder, brown boys who seem to float
Over nails, cracked glass. Blood's inevitable, grin
Of corpses in the moss, but up Gravel Mountain
Barefooted fathers smite rock to axes, goad
Daughters to crawl his culverts, leap his fence,
Stealth in shadows to steal bullion or just a tin
Of milk from stoked larders, a plump chicken
To roast on scrap iron, bleach or brine to rinse
Fresh wounds, then slip before daylight can seep
Through the cold panes, his only child asleep
On goose down, a pink bed, a unicorn that neighs
When pinched, her lace doll with the purple beret.

Our Lord of Miracles

Lima, late 1960s

October is the month sea-clouds dye desert skies
Violet and eight men in purple suits bear,
Dead march, Christ's bier: one ton filigreed silver,
Solid or gilt, as trombones moan, a cornet cries

Off key, twined roses tumble from windows,
The cortege of thousands swaying to thuribles,
Spices mixed with squatters' dust, gray foothills
Of the Andean poor. Tallow spatters, elbows

Knock my face, bruising an eye, purple-robed
Women who totter with candles, praying the flame
Doesn't die by sweat or tears, a flash of mayhem,
Who fear the trivial mishap that could bode

Disaster anytime; so they, like Mamá, bargain
For favors with *promesas*, their litany of barter—
Give me this and I'll do that—murmured to a purr.
The pious poor crawl, knees bruised to gain

A tad more grace, which Mamá, a staid *doña*, calls
Vulgar. Then the city shakes, the bier reels,
Bearers topple, lines break, dogs yowl, chapel veils
On fire, flakes of scalp afloat, rose petals.

My fingers crack in her grip when a rogue bus
Veers into the crowd, and Mamá, high-heeled, twists
An ankle, falls on a legless beggar, leather fists
Pushing a dolly, her dress torn, beehive mussed.

She moans my name, gropes the ground, torso
Caught on the dolly, beggar's head a rock.
Limbs squeeze me like pincers. I cannot walk
Or speak, pray in scraps, garble words I know

From catechism. I hear the crack of truncheons.
A water cannon fires. Crowds cram into alleys,
Vestibules. Cops rescue the survivors, our pleas
Heard, Mamá would say; those with mortal sins,

Though, trucked to the morgue. Our bodies heal.
I return to school, soccer; Mamá wilts in her room,
Smoky, a convent of candles, fearing the doom
Of pride, praying all day, scattering rice to kneel.

Top

Despite solvents' fog, red sawdust that itched like mites,
Papá's factory had whirly augurs, big hammers to peen
Turpentine drums, foam bins to dive, steel springs' trampoline.
A staple-gun outlaw, I'd draw fast, aim the notched sights
To spray dusty men who'd rather grin than spank
The *patrón*'s son. At my whim, they bent down to prune
Lumber's decay & lathe a top, nail-tipped, cut with moon,
Sun, stars, trim's golden string I wound tight to yank,
Spin everywhere, even Mass and English class.
Until the schoolmaster trampled on recess, his strap
A tongue of tacks, the phone call, hoarse, censorious,
That made Mamá send me to bed with dry bread, a glass
Of water. Belt in hand, Papá roused me, no strain or fuss
As he took count, my legs wet, hands gripping his lap.

Toro

Q-tips for horns, a leather tail for my wool
Shorts, I moo, charge till the sweet *chicha* jug
Spills on the parquet, slicks our roped bull-
Ring of twill chairs, & Carlos slides on the rug,
His cape, a red scarf, hung on a stick. I crawl
Fast, gathering strength for victory's snort, trot,
& gore, sure his mop stick won't get the final
Thrust. Then my head, thrashing, hits a squat
Divan, & the Q-tip punctures my right ear,
Pulsing so much I writhe on the floor, cry, blare.
Mamá rushes to bale me in blankets. We tear
Away to Dr. Ruiz who straps me to a chair,
Drips ether, squirts oil, lubes a tube, his weird
Gadget sucking out fluid into a glass sphere.

Breakfast with Capitalists

Their favorite café like a baroque wedding cake
Of spumoni marble and gypsum marzipan,
Waiters in glazed frocks quick to placate the don
With a peeve, expatriates like Papá who rake
Dollars off the books with bribes, the fixed trade.
Sipping espresso, eyeing the paper, they talk
Money, politics, their dread of some slight havoc
Priming revolution. Discord comes, a grenade
Of insult tossed. Short Papá stands on a chair
To quell his cadre; busboys dab spills and stains.
As I doodle melted butter, their anger wanes,
And the talk turns to me, his first son, the heir
Who'll log the Amazon, mine the Andes, fish
The Pacific, conquest by capital, laws to vanquish.

Juancito's Wake

Lost Grove Squatters' Camp, Lima, 1985

Over white vinyl, Rosa sets silver
candlesticks (rented), tinplate crucifixes—
five solder wounds—son's coffin
trembling on crippled legs when an old truck
rumbles past these desert shacks,

cardboard & reed mats tied to sticks.
Daughter Rosita crosses herself the Spanish
way, kissing the thumb when done,
pins purple-cloth medals of El Niño Jesús,
a burial gown sewn from rice sacking.

Mourners will come with egg-bread angels,
Our Lord of Sorrows' pudding—purple corn—
for the afterlife; most are live-out maids
like Rosa, the rest laundresses who twist shirts
until they surrender those last waterdrops

too precious for dirt, saved in oil drums
used to wash dishes & newborns. Dead from
hunger, Juancito is the third child she's lost
since coming from Ancash, highland province
in *la mancha india*, Perú's poorest.

They pose in Sunday's clothes, Rosa stoic,
dignified; in the background a road map

of Perú, one square clock that doesn't work.
Juancito's rubbery hands hold daisies,
shredded newspaper smelling of fish meal.

I take out a can from my bandoleer,
shoot from angles, cropping for dramatic
composition. Images freeze in silver;
flash mummifies. "Third World people
are real," customers say

as they buy $1,000 prints—poster size
Agfa sepia, Cibachrome color—to be hung
beneath track lights, Bal Harbour & South Beach
condos. The last reel shot, I thank Rosa,
handing her rubber-banded bills

she buries inside a broken bottle
of *pisco* shaped like an Inca figurine.
"It's for her I struggle. Already she knows
how to read & write, do arithmetic."
Holding the sheet-metal door open,

Rosita rubs rheum off black eyes
like wilted grapes—asks, "In your
country are there many poor like
here?" "Poverty is relative," I answer
stupidly, leaving her puzzled.

Girls hopscotch along hedgerows
of barbed wire, runts bark at garbage sparks.
I return to the hotel, the cab having waited two

hours. "These are the children God forgot,"
cabbie says, hissing away barefoot boys,

shoe-shine boxes strapped to their backs,
pockets bulging with rags that buff leather
into obsidian mirrors. Yelling *señor*,
señor, they run through a wake
of dust, the incense of cloudless skies.

Notes for Poems

"Courtyard of Clotheslines, Angel Hill"

Eleggua is one of the major divinities of Santería, a syncretic Cuban religion of Yoruba origin.

"Aubade: The Charcoal Makers"

Shot in the Italian neo-realist style of the postwar period, *El Mégano* was directed by Julio García Espinosa in collaboration with Tomás Gutierrez Alea, Alfredo Guevara, and José Massip. During its first screening at the University of Havana, it was confiscated by the police of Fulgencio Batista.

"*Spiderman* in Havana"

The theater was noisy and full when I saw this movie in December of 2002 at Cine La Rampa, right across from the Habana Hilton.

"Village of the Water People"

The small mountain community of *Los Acúaticos*, or the Water People, consists of the remaining followers of Antoñica, a peasant woman once revered as a miraculous water healer in 1930's Pinar del Río. The Cuban director Manuel Octavio Gómez filmed in 1971 a semi-fictional account of her life, entitled *Los días del agua* (Days of Water).

"Pyx"

Soon after arriving to the United States in 2002, my adoptive daughter Valerie (then age 3) was diagnosed with severe attention-deficit hyperactivity disorder (ADHD).

"Adderall"

Commonly used to treat ADHD, Adderall is a stimulant consisting of four kinds of amphetamine.

"The Gringo Called Ñakak"

I first learned of the ñakak, also called *pishtako* in Quechua, from Nicholas Shakespeare's 1994 documentary *Return to the Sacred Ice*. The Peruvian writer Mario Vargas Llosa writes of this creature as well in his short novel *Death in the Andes* (1996).

"Altiplano"

This poem is based in part on footage of the market at the foot of Perú's Mt. Ausangate (during the Festival of Qoyllur Rit'i) in *Return to the Sacred Ice*.

"The Devil's Miner"

This poem is inspired by a 2005 documentary of the same name, directed by Kief Davidson and Richard Ladkani, which tells the life of Basilio Vargas, a fourteen-year-old Bolivian miner. During colonial times, Cerro Potosí (Potosí Mountain) was the principal source of silver ore for the Spanish Empire. The phrase *vale un* (worth a) *Potosí* denotes wealth or fortune.

Glossary

amorcito	A term of endearment, diminutive for love.
bacalao	Dried codfish.
bambú	Bamboo.
cachumbambé	A Cuban onomatopoeia for seesaw.
caoba	Mahogany.
cariñito	Another term of endearment, equivalent to honey.
castizo	Pure Spanish.
cerro	Highland. *Serranos(as)* are highlanders.
chicha	An alcoholic beverage made from purple corn. Also non-alcoholic.
corúa	Cormorant.
cuora	Spanish pronunciation of quarter.
El Cristo de Piedra	Stone Christ.
guaracha	A popular form of Cuban music.
guayaba	Guava.
guayacán	Cuban name of the lignum vitae (wood of life).
jagüey	Cuban name of the strangler fig.
La Sagüesera	The southwest area of Little Havana.
la Bolita	The Puerto Rican lottery, illegal in Florida. Literally the "little ball."
manglar negro	Black mangrove.
más bulbos	More bulbs.

mátalo ya	Kill it now.
no puedo	I can't.
patrón	Equivalent to owner or boss but with the suggestion of master.
picadura	Finely cut tobacco.
pisco	A type of Peruvian brandy.
retablo	Retable.
Sol	Perú's national currency. Literally the sun.
traif	Trash, not kosher in Yiddish.
quipus	Knotted strings used by the Incas for counting.
shekinah	A Talmudic term for God's physical presence on Earth.
yagruma	Cuban name of the trumpet tree.
zafra	Sugar harvest.
zunzún	Echoic name of the common hummingbird of Cuba.

To order or obtain more information on these or other University of Nebraska Press titles, visit www.nebraskapress.unl.edu.

CPSIA information can be obtained at www.ICGtesting.com
Printed in the USA
BVOW020533030713

324929BV00001B/2/P